Veterinarians

Community Workers

by Lucia Raatma

Content Adviser: Robin Downing, D.V.M.,
Windsor, Colorado

Reading Adviser: Dr. Linda D. Labbo,
College of Education, Department of Reading Education,
The University of Georgia

COMPASS POINT BOOKS

Minneapolis, Minnesota

Compass Point Books
3109 West 50th Street, #115
Minneapolis, MN 55410

Visit Compass Point Books on the Internet at *www.compasspointbooks.com* or e-mail your request to *custserv@compasspointbooks.com*

Photographs ©: PhotoDisc, cover; Index Stock/Kent Knudson, 4; Norvia Behling, 5, 6, 7, 8, 11, 14, 15, 21, 22, 23, 24, 25, 26; Ron Spomer/Visuals Unlimited, 9; Photo Network, 10; Wolfgang Kaehler/Corbis, 12; Richard T. Nowitz/Corbis, 13; William J. Weber/Visuals Unlimited, 16; Kent & Donna Dannen, 17, 27; Unicorn Stock Photos/Alon Reininger, 18; Bob Krist/Corbis, 19; Unicorn Stock Photos/Jim Shippee, 20.

Editors: E. Russell Primm, Emily J. Dolbear, and Pam Rosenberg
Photo Researcher: Svetlana Zhurkina
Photo Selector: Linda S. Koutris
Designer: Bradfordesign, Inc.

Library of Congress Cataloging-in-Publication Data

Raatma, Lucia.
   Veterinarians / by Lucia Raatma ; reading adviser, Linda D. Labbo.
      p. cm. — (Community workers)
   Includes bibliographical references and index.
   Summary: Introduces the work of doctors of veterinary medicine, including duties, training, skills needed, and contribution to the community.
   ISBN 0-7565-0304-3 (hardcover)
   ISBN 0-7565-1198-4 (paperback)
      1. Veterinarians—Juvenile literature. 2. Veterinary medicine—Vocational guidance—Juvenile literature.
[1. Veterinarians. 2. Occupations.] I. Title. II. Series.
   SF756 .R225 2002
   636.089'092—dc21   2002002955

Table of Contents

What Do Veterinarians Do?

Veterinarians are doctors who take care of animals. They are often called "vets." They help sick animals get better. They also help animals stay well. Vets often help animals give birth to their young. Some vets do medical **research**. This means they look for new ways to help animals.

A veterinarian greets a dog.

A veterinarian examines a cat.

What Tools and Equipment Do They Use?

Vets and **physicians** use the same kinds of equipment. Does your cat have a fever? The vet uses a thermometer to find out the cat's temperature. Maybe your dog has cut his leg. The vet cleans the cut. Then she covers it with a bandage.

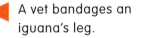
A vet bandages an iguana's leg.

A thermometer is used to check a cat's temperature.

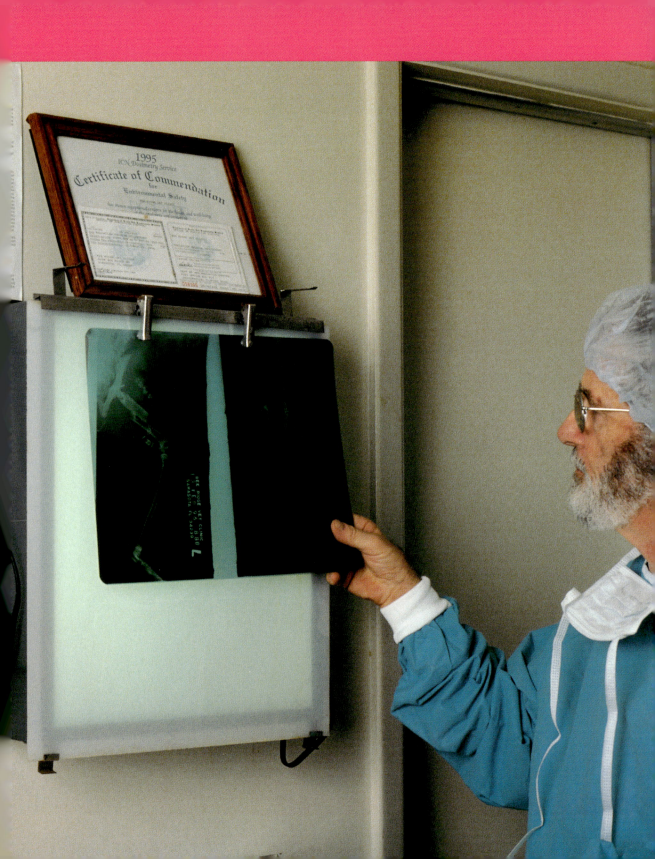

Using **X-ray machines** helps vets see if an animal has a broken bone. A **stethoscope** helps the vet listen to an animal's heart and lungs. Sometimes animals need **surgery** to get better. Vets use small, sharp knives called scalpels to do surgery.

A veterinarian uses an X ray to look for broken bones.

A vet uses a stethoscope to listen to a bear cub's breathing and heartbeat.

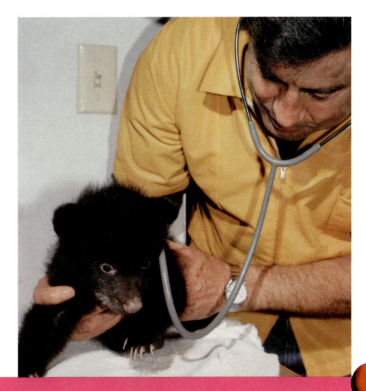

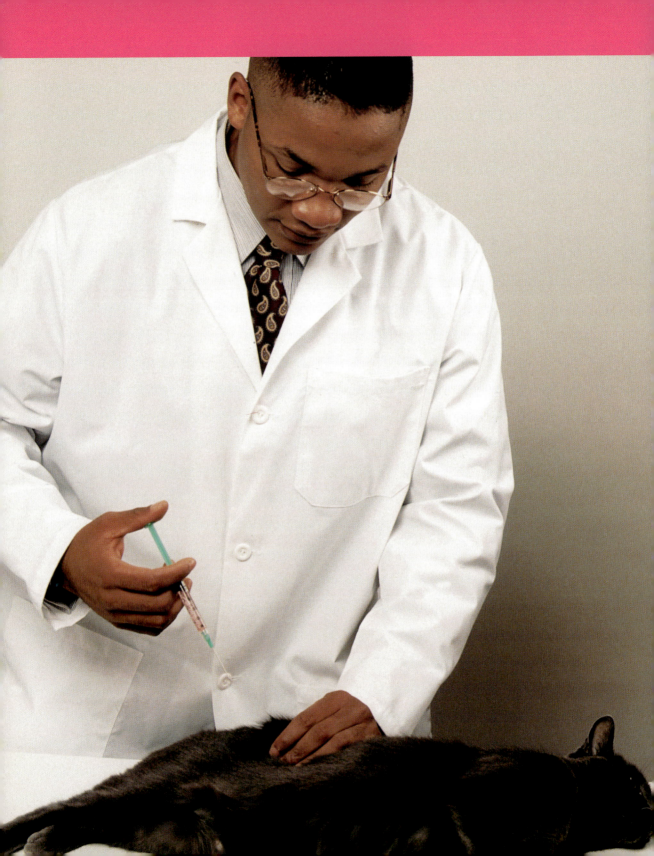

How Do Veterinarians Help?

Veterinarians help keep our animals healthy. They **vaccinate** animals against **diseases**. Some animal diseases can spread to humans. **Rabies** is one of these diseases. Healthy animals help people keep healthy, too. Vets also teach pet owners how to care for their pets.

A vet gives a cat a shot.

A vet discusses pet care with a dog owner.

Where Do Veterinarians Work?

Many vets work in animal hospitals. These hospitals are a lot like your doctor's office and hospital. Some vets work on farms and in zoos. Other vets work in animal shelters. Vets who do medical research work in **laboratories**. Some vets work for the army or navy. Some vets even work at the circus!

◀ A vet gives a llama a shot.

A vet cares for a dolphin at an aquarium. ▶

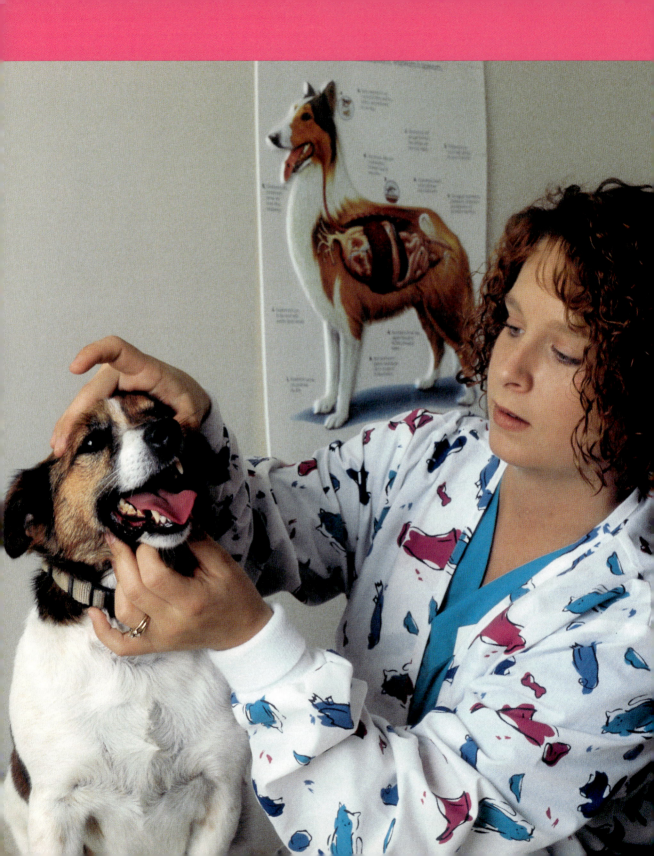

With Whom Do Veterinarians Work?

Vets work with animals. Sometimes these animals are hurt, frightened, or sick. Veterinary technicians and veterinary assistants help vets take care of animals. Receptionists do the office work. Vets also work with pet owners. They help people make decisions about their pets.

A veterinary technician checks a dog's teeth.

The vet and cockatiel's owner work together to clip the bird's nails.

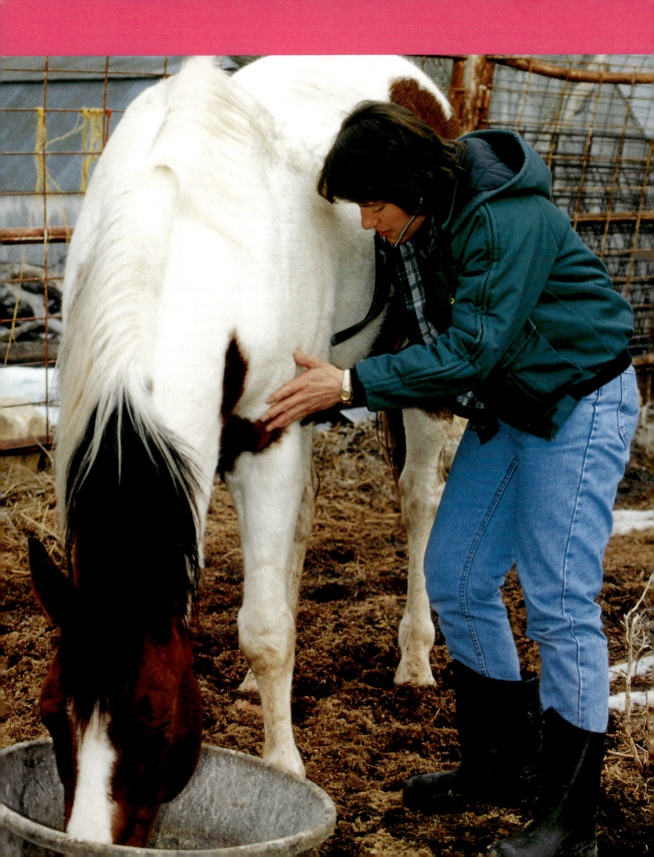

What Do Veterinarians Wear?

Veterinarians usually wear medical coats over their own clothes. They wear hospital pants and shirts when they do surgery. Vets who work on farms or zoos often wear sturdier clothes. They wear coveralls and heavy shoes or boots to work with large animals.

Some veterinarians work with large animals such as horses.

Sometimes veterinarians must perform surgery on pets.

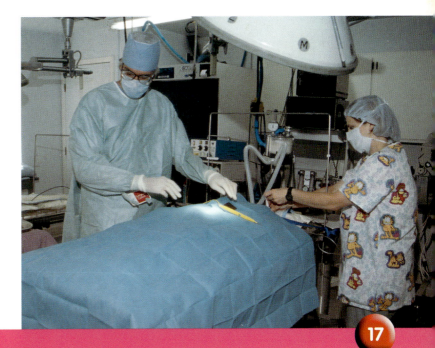

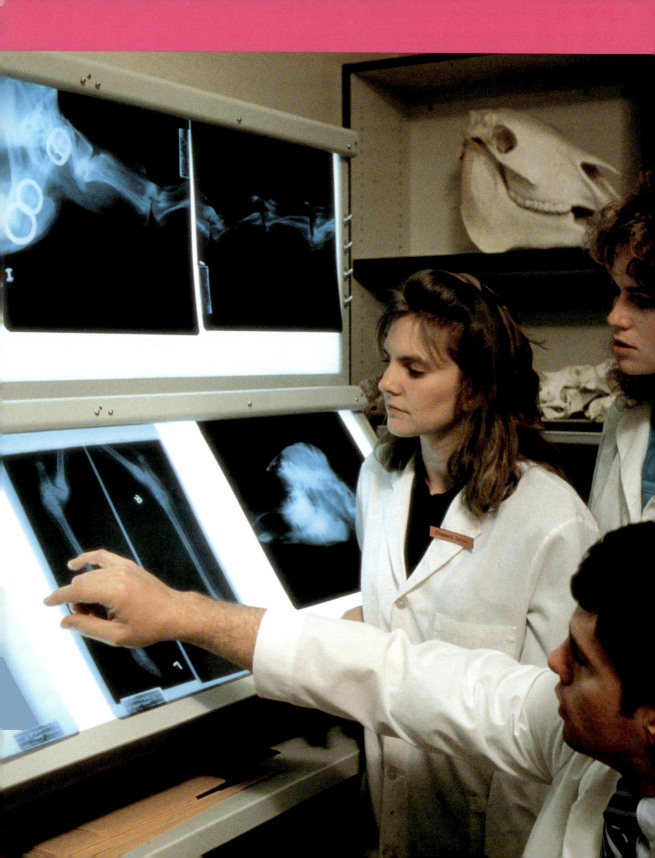

What Training Does It Take?

If you want to be a vet you must go to college. After graduating from college, you will go to a veterinary college. It is not easy to get into a veterinary college, however. Good grades are important. Science courses such as biology and chemistry are also needed. It takes a lot of hard work to become a veterinarian.

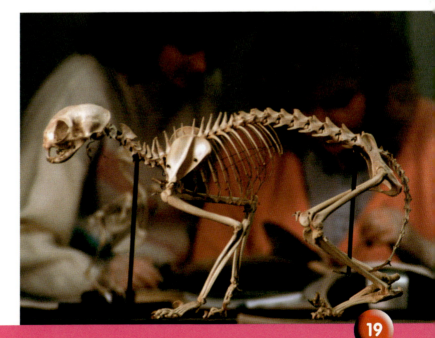

◀ These students are training to be veterinarians.

Studying a cat skeleton helps students learn about cats. ▶

What Skills Do They Need?

Veterinarians must have respect for animals. A good vet has a calm, gentle manner. Vets must know how to take care of all kinds of animals. They must also be good at working with all kinds of people. They work with the owners and trainers of the animals.

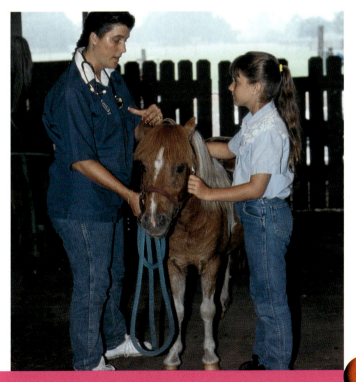

Veterinarians use drugs to help animals get well.

A veterinarian teaches a girl how to care for her pony.

What Problems Do They Face?

Most vets work long hours. They often take care of animals on weekends and late at night. Farm and zoo vets may have to travel a lot. A frightened animal may hurt a vet. Sometimes veterinarians can't help an animal get well. This can be sad for the vet as well as the animal's owner.

◄ Some veterinarians travel to farms to treat animals.

An otter gets a shot to help him stay healthy. ▶

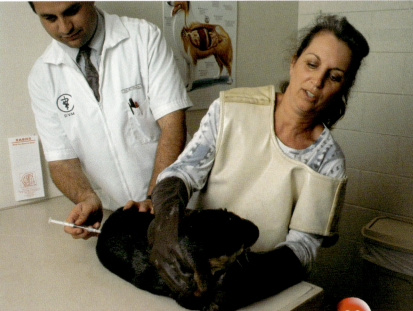

Would You Like to Be a Veterinarian?

Are science and math among your best subjects? Do you enjoy being around animals? Maybe being a vet is right for you. You can start to prepare now. Offer to help neighbors and friends take care of their pets. Try to visit farms and zoos.

◀ A girl takes care of her injured cat.

It is fun to pretend to be a veterinarian. ▶

A Veterinarian's Tools and Clothes

pet owner

stethoscope

bandages

examining table

cat

lab coat

At the Animal Hospital

pet owner

receptionist

computer

reception desk

dog

A Veterinarian's Day

Early Morning

- The vet arrives at the animal hospital. She checks the day's schedule with the receptionist.
- The vet performs surgery on a sick cat.

Noon

- The vet attends a community lunch. There she gives a talk on pet licensing and rabies vaccines.

Afternoon

- The vet talks to a family that has just adopted a puppy. She gives the puppy a checkup and offers advice to the new pet owners.
- Later in the day, the vet meets with the veterinary assistants and orders necessary supplies for the animal hospital.

Evening

- The vet goes home for dinner.
- Later, the vet returns to the hospital to check on the cat that had surgery earlier in the day. The cat stays in the hospital overnight.

Night

- The vet receives an emergency call about an injured hawk found on the side of the road. She returns to the office and examines the hawk. She sets the hawk's broken wing and keeps the bird overnight.
- In the morning she will find a zoo willing to care for the wounded bird.

Glossary

diseases—sicknesses

laboratories—places where people study and experiment with special equipment

physicians—doctors who take care of people

rabies—a virus carried by animals that can be deadly

research—to investigate and collect facts about something

stethoscope—a medical tool used by doctors to listen to breathing and heartbeats

surgery—a medical operation

vaccinate—to give a shot of medicine in order to prevent disease

X-ray machines—machines that take pictures of the bones and organs inside the body

Did You Know?

- The United States has twenty-seven colleges of veterinary medicine. Canada has four such colleges.

- Only about half of the students who apply to veterinary school are accepted.

- Some veterinarians work for the United States Department of Agriculture. They help make sure that our food is safe to eat and comes from healthy animals.

- In some countries, veterinary technicians are called veterinary nurses.

Want to Know More?

At the Library

Ermitage, Kathleen. *Veterinarian*. Austin, Tex.: Raintree/Steck-Vaughn, 2000.

Leonard, Marcia. *The Pet Vet*. Brookfield, Conn.: Millbrook Press, 1999.

Ready, Dee. *Veterinarians*. Mankato, Minn.: Bridgestone Books, 1997.

Walker-Hodge, Judith. *Animal Hospital*. New York: DK Publishing, 1999.

On the Web

American Veterinary Medical Association Kids Korner

http://www.avma.org/care4pets/avmakids.htm

For information about taking care of pets and finding out more about careers in veterinary medicine

The Brookfield Zoo

http://www.brookfieldzoo.org/

For pictures of and information about many kinds of animals

Through the Mail

American Veterinary Medical Association

1931 North Meacham Road, Suite 100

Schaumburg, IL 60173

For information about veterinary careers

On the Road

San Diego Zoo

2920 Zoo Drive

San Diego, CA 92101

691/234-3153

To see an amazing collection of animals and learn about the people who take care of them

Index

About the Author

Lucia Raatma received her bachelor's degree in English literature from the University of South Carolina and her master's degree in cinema studies from New York University. She has written a wide range of books for young people. When she is not researching or writing, she enjoys going to movies, playing tennis, practicing yoga, and spending time with her husband, daughter, and golden retriever. She lives in New York.